ANIMALS OF AFRICA
COLORING BOOK

Carlo Atzei

1. Savanna

Animal species: African bush elephant (Loxodonta africana), blue wildebeest (Connochaetes taurinus), plains zebra (Equus quagga), ground pangolin (Smutsia temminckii)

2. Hippos
Animal species: hippopotamus (Hippopotamus amphibius), red-billed oxpecker (Buphagus erythrorhynchus), black-headed heron (Ardea melanocephala)

3. Sahara Desert
Animal species: dromedary (Camelus dromedarius), fennec fox (Vulpes zerda), common sandfish (Scincus scincus), deathstalker scorpion (Leiurus quinquestriatus)

4. Lions
Animal species: lion (Panthera leo)

5. Madagascar

Animal species: ring-tailed lemur (Lemur catta), Madagascan fruit bat (Eidolon dupreanum), comet moth (Argema mittrei), Rainbow Milkweed Locust, (Phymateus saxosus), Madagascar hissing cockroach (Gromphadorhina portentosa)

6. Giraffe
Animal species: South African giraffe (Giraffa camelopardalis giraffa)

7. Rhino and Gazelles
Animal species: black rhinoceros (Diceros bicornis), Thomson's gazelle (Eudorcas thomsonii), yellow-billed stork (Mycteria ibis), Verreaux's eagle-owl (Bubo lacteus), African hoopoe (Upupa africana), black mamba (Dendroaspis polylepis)

8. Leopard, Python and Hornbill
Animal species: leopard (Panthera pardus) , African rock python (Python sebae),
southern yellow-billed hornbill (Tockus leucomelas)

9. Namibia

Animal species: gemsbok (Oryx gazella), spotted hyena (Crocuta crocuta), common ostrich (Struthio camelus), secretary bird (Sagittarius serpentarius), black-necked spitting cobra (Naja nigricollis)

10. Gorilla
Animal species: western gorilla (Gorilla gorilla), Janetta Themis forester (Euphaedra
janetta), Angola white lady (Graphium angolanus), black-kneed duskhawker
(Gynacantha bullata)

11. Ituri Rainforest

Animal species: okapi (Okapia johnstoni), water chevrotain (Hyemoschus aquaticus), Hamlyn's monkey (Cercopithecus hamlyni), Congo peafowl (Afropavo congensis), Ituri batis (Batis ituriensis)

12. Bateleur Eagle
Animal species: Bateleur (Terathopius ecaudatus)

13. Caracal
Animal species: caracal (Caracal caracal), helmeted chameleon (Trioceros hoehnelii)

14. Wet Season
Animal species: Cape buffalo (Syncerus caffer), plain grass frog (Ptychadena anchietae), giant African land snail (Achatina fulica)

15. Mother and Cubs
Animal species: cheetah (Acinonyx jubatus), African savanna hare (Lepus victoriae), African civet (Civettictis civetta), aardvark (Orycteropus afer), Wahlberg's epauletted fruit bat (Epomophorus wahlbergi), herald snake (Crotaphopeltis hotamboeia), baboon spider (Pelinobius muticus)

16. Under the Baobab

Animal species: common eland (Taurotragus oryx), Grant's gazelle (Nanger granti), African wild dog (Lycaon pictus), common warthog (Phacochoerus africanus), leopard tortoise (Stigmochelys pardalis), grey crowned crane (Balearica regulorum), Von der Decken's hornbill (Tockus deckeni), southern ground hornbill (Bucorvus leadbeateri)

17. Addax
Animal species: addax (Addax nasomaculatus), Sahara sand viper (Cerastes vipera)

18. Serengeti

Animal species: serval (Leptailurus serval), Kirk's dik-dik (Madoqua kirkii), aardwolf (Proteles cristata), bat-eared fox (Otocyon megalotis), sable antelope (Hippotragus niger), waterbuck (Kobus ellipsiprymnus), yellow baboon (Papio cynocephalus), rainbow agama (Agama agama), helmeted guineafowl (Numida meleagris), long-crested eagle (Lophaetus occipitalis), Fischer's lovebird (Agapornis fischeri)

19. Tsingy de Bemaraha
Animal species: fossa (Cryptoprocta ferox), tailless tenrec (Tenrec ecaudatus),
Madagascan harrier-hawk (Polyboroides radiatus)

20. By the Water
Animal species: greater kudu (Tragelaphus strepsiceros), impala (Aepyceros melampus), Nile crocodile (Crocodylus niloticus), marabou stork (Leptoptilos crumenifer), malachite kingfisher (Corythornis cristatus)

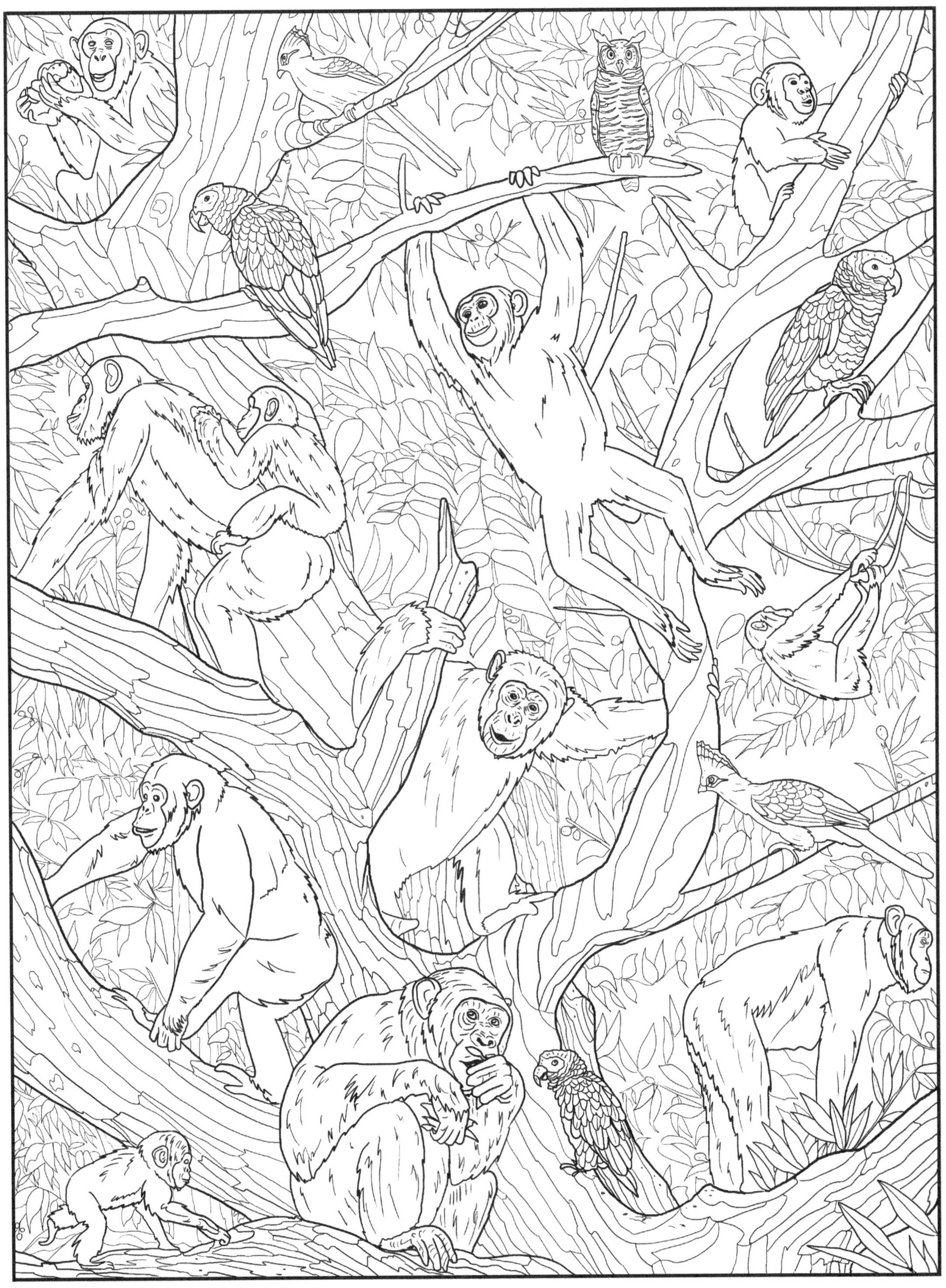

21. Life Among Trees
Animal species: chimpanzee (Pan troglodytes), grey parrot (Psittacus erithacus), black-billed turaco (Tauraco schuettii), Fraser's eagle-owl (Bubo poensis)

22. Tropical Rainforest
Animal species: mandrill (Mandrillus sphinx), white-crested turaco (Tauraco leucolophus), red-chested owlet (Glaucidium tephronotum), Gaboon viper (Bitis gabonica), emperor scorpion (Pandinus imperator)

23. Vultures and Jackals
Animal species: white-backed vulture (Gyps africanus), side-striped jackal (Lupulella adusta)

24. Tiny Animals of Africa

Animal species: Striped grass mouse (Lemniscomys zebra),giant African millipede (Archispirostreptus gigas), gaudy commodore (Precis octavia), Scheffler's dwarf gecko (Lygodactylus scheffleri), ladybug (Cheilomenes lunata)

25. Meerkats

Animal species: meerkat (Suricata suricatta)